SOUL OF WONDERS

POEMS SPEAK WORLD'S TRUTHS

Y N SHYLOCK

Made with ❤ on the Notion Press Platform
www.notionpress.com

What ever I ***'YN Shylock'*** write on a paper it is always dedicated to that part of nature who blessed me with the oppertunity to write. Then my works are dedicated to that holy soul who gave me this very thought and power to emphasize on world's way of thoughts.

At last this book is dedicated to you

Contents

1. The Enormous Nature 1

2. Nature's Reprisal 2

3. Scientific Nature 4

4. Those Days 5

5. Mistakes Happen 7

6. My Way There 9

7. Pain Of Care 11

8. Death 13

9. Lonely Everything 14

10. Loving World 15

Thank You 17

1. The Enormous Nature

Wow! the earth is a great feature,
it is the magic of the nature.
You can see greenary everywhere,
you need to take care.

The places you never saw,
and we can never see,
these birds come here and make beautiful sounds,
which we can hear as loud as far as the ground.

The rushing stream,
which always comes in our dreams.
You have an endless pit
of nature,
which we hit
and kill it by our own hands.

You have to save nature,
thats your best feature.
If you cut trees
then what about your frees.

2. Nature's Reprisal

Just ago a few days,
along the happy ways;
there were ground,
which were bound to sounds!

Kids used to play all day long;
when this pandemic started its song!.
The cries of man,
have started the ban.
Even then! we all are united!
unitedly working for the country delighted.

The end of men was a turn for the burn;
when the world started to learn-
Only the nature......
whould save all its creatures.
Only if they were sorrow,
for the deeds they borrow;
tomorrow would be a turn,
if the world would learn-
"the need of one,
was the deed of someone................"

let's see,
what the world would be.
but!, my prayers for nature.....
are 'to save all its creatures.................'.

3. Scientific Nature

Nature was once a don,
when science was learned-
it got upon
and burned
the dead remains of the sun.

Seems not possible but can always be done
never the less it was what we earned.
that little you were the hope of world uprun.
the day when you entreat the world as your son,
sun shined with more flames upon.

you got life,
it got smile.....
world is your slave
hats off to you science!!

4. Those Days

Ever thought who you were?
this you was not the you there.
For sure i can say
siting at the shiny bay,
those days all were so well-
tinkling with the temple bell.

those days where god himself was gay,
looking at the smlies that sway.
none than you
can get back the few,
waiting for you
never the new.

small lifes with farms and hay,
the cattle used to say:
you the mighty are
all the mighty were.
when those days flash back in eyes,
a little drop of tear lies-
down my face on the land,
that flash rinses upon the sand.

those days can ever be back,
those days can never be back!

5. Mistakes Happen

Now when I leave this world,
go so far as such never told.
I miss your words that say,
you are not fit for the way.
God please,
let it ease.
let me go back to find someone waiting for me,
pacient and calm-
that one day i would charm.
Know it would never happen,
but few hopes just got rippen;
what if!may be!
you change,
my brain thought in range.
Alas it can never happen,
rippen fruits just get rotten.
you know what?
dreams are good
but they can never lend you food.
Mistakes happen!
by you, by me -
can't you forgive?

Mistakes happen!
why don't you forgive?
Today you feel burned!
but see tomorrow can make you turned.
never lose people for small key
May be tomorrow can be what you hope for.
See what god gives.
may be ! if possible!
inform me too about it.
Mistakes happen!
wont you forgive?
I TRUST YOU

6. My Way There

School was a temple
where people used to rumble.
Talk, talk for which I was on the rock.
kept out it was fun looking at the clock-
seeing when to get back
to set back my rack.
friends all around
screaming in weird sound;
never can I forget those few
always being something new.
now that I have to go,
leave my school with a greateful bow.
so sad to miss all those-
eyes with tears, hands with rose.
so sad to miss hose deeds I owe
my debts left to memories in row.
leaving things not memories
i go with golden flees:
friends knowledge and keys
to get myself in better ease.
The way I chose now,
is so differnt but how?

it is the way to heaven,
through hell crossing oceans seven.
Tomorrow I will be back
showing the world my hack,
to kill small clashes
go up into ashes.
I assure myself of me
tomorrow I will be here with glee-
shining not like a star in the sky
but like the sun uphigh.

7. Pain Of Care

Never can we understand,
love mingled in such a strand.
schold but love,
care but how?
let me explain
how the sun shined in rain!
love tinged with anger as venture
we named a creature as teacher.
taught me how to survive
in the lonely last life alive.
it sometimes hurts
but always fades in dirts.
it was I who thought
it got myself to rot.
but,never did it so-
i left debts to teachers though.
never ask you to let great gain,
leave them in that rich rain.
but always faced the pain-
to see your great gain.
so i feel the pain?
no! it was love as acid ain.

it hurts but fine,
they just wanted us to shine.
now when I realise that love
I shiver to death but how?
let me explain
how the star sunk in rain?
criticized, back talked,
but always thought they are kids not to be blocked.
kids commented,
but that creatures love still was tinted.
now when I realise the sins I borrow,
i feel so sorrow.
but when you say " my child,
I love you, even though you were wild".
My heart starts to melt
for what now I felt.
hate turned as love?
or an angel disguised so now?

8. Death

few things haunt
like holy fire under want,
so do this thing haunt
such a pleasure i would never want.
death was it chasing me,
saying I dont need the life to be-
myself not thee,
so now I am going with glee.
today here
tomorrow there
never am I stable on the weir-
going to hell up there.
death calls me
to go with glee,
so now I die
to go with joy.
deaths calls me
god chases me
so I have to go
A river of Death as flow.

9. Lonely Everything

I found someone
for whom I was everyone.
somtimes we'd fight
but this time it was light.
something which I dint expect
happend to be such a theft.
now I wander
just to wonder
is it me?
or something else so free?
not one would bother?
did my brain think rather?
think of something
which was never everything.
something always matters,
the way my tear flatters-
just can tell all of it,
why do you have to go for it?
helpless hands ask for help,
selfless brain ask for itself,
but me going down-
asked for something as my own.

10. Loving World

I thought world was wrong,
no it was right-
I wasn't so strong
it wasn't so straight.
now, I thing I was wrong,
the was love was rained...
it was so strong,
love with care was stained.
I started to move for you
searching for something new.
I learned you care-
when I just started to stare.
Isn't this world so different
ir was it all I could see through the vent?
shine like a star
spread your light so far.
got to know people care,
this made my eyes flood
on the floor with foot all bare,
love that boiled your blood,
love that smiles over your head.

Thank You

this is a loving thanks for patiently reading this whole book

if you can relate with these poems I would feel so happy

few speak about your life where as others speak on how people i.e world treats you and your feelings.

something always hurts but you never have to cry for it

just listen to your mind it is saying to learn for it.

by the way I am going to publish another book sooner with ten more poems so keep calm and enjoy being yourself till then .

YN Shylock signing off.

Printed by Libri Plureos GmbH in Hamburg, Germany